words about y o u

tye ballew

words about you

for Chris,
without you
I wouldn't have these words

I wanted this
To be simple and sweet
Just enough
To capture the beauty you
Bring into this world
Bring into my world

These are my
words about you

Spent the night
On the floor
And smiled
Because I dreamt
Of you

It’s the taste
Of your skin
Soft skin
I miss when you’re
Not next to me

He has galaxies in his eyes and
I can’t help but wish on the shooting
Stars I see

It’s cliché and probably
Worn out but I get the
Most beautiful butterflies
Whenever you’re around

You found me in my
Bedroom whispering
Ghost stories into the dark
Alone
You sat down to listen until
There were no more left to hear

The moments between sleep
Is when you creep in
And push me
Back into the blissful abyss

I don’t need to dream
To find what
I’ve been looking for
With you
My reality is better

I’m not so lonely
When my lips
Are against your
Two thighs

Sometimes
In the quiet between
Your breaths
I can hear your heart
And I know
That it's mine

Long after you're gone I
Hope you still haunt my
Sweetest dreams

Tonight the moon
Is full
Like my heart
The moment you
Walked into the room

This morning
The fog hangs low
Like I hang my hopes
And I wonder
What it is about me
That makes you stay

For once I want to be
The stars that sparkle
In your eyes
For once I want
To be the gravitational pull
That draws you in
I want to be
The sun that shines
Behind your lips
For once
I want to be the
Center of someone's universe

As the autumn breeze
Ruffles my hair
I wonder if your thoughts
Are consumed by me like
Mine are of you

You're the one thing my
Head and heart
Have agreed on

my mind changes
like the seasons

Life was brought back
To me the moment
Your lips met mine
Finally
I could breathe again

I could scream
But I don’t think
You’d hear me
Because your eyes
Are deaf to everything
I lay in front of you

You said you'd be a thief
You'd steal my heart in the
Dead of night
But how can you steal something
I'm so willing to give you

take it

It’s the way you
Light up a room when
You walk in
Or the way your eyes
Crinkle when you smile
It’s the way you
Not only hold me
With your hands but
Also with your love

Let me
Be
The only
One

You were the first shot the
First bullet to the heart after I tasted
Death and I want nothing more than
For you to take me out

Sometimes I wonder
Why it is
The way it is
And why I feel
The way I feel
But other times I wonder
If you feel the same
Way I feel or
If I feel too deep

When I see roses
Pastel pinks and creams
I think back
To when the drugs
That ran through my veins
Were the lights
That reflected from your eyes
And that's the moment
I knew
I would never lay eyes
On something as
Beautiful as you

I know that
Deep down my heart
Is falling and
I can’t make it stop
Please tell me that
You’ll catch me before
Gravity does

Maybe you're my sun and I'm
Your Icarus but even when the sun
Sets I see you in the stars and
Still I want to fly to steal a closer look
Maybe I won't fall
Maybe you'll catch me before
The waves do

It’s the way
The morning hits
When you’re in my bed
How you hold me
With your eyes
Like you’ve never
Seen something so beautiful

I’m not scared
To end up alone
I’d rather just not
End up without you
Because you bring
Better days and
Warmer nights
And I don’t want to
Miss out on what
Forever
Could feel like
With you

If there’s one thing
I know
It’s that you
Feel like home

When I say I love you
I don't say it like
Others say it as a place holder
I say I love you from the
Deepest part of my being
When I say I love you
I surrender every ounce
Of myself to you
My darkness and my light
In hopes I find you in both
I say I love you because
I see constellations in your eyes
And by them I can find
My way home
That's what I mean
When I say I love you

It’s been 24 hours
Since you said *I love you*
The words bounced off
The lights and they were all
I could see
And in that moment I wanted
To see nothing more
It’s been 24 hours

I want to be the words
That dance on your tongue
The words you speak
In the quiet of night
The words you share
Between friends when
I'm not around
I want to be the words
That form the smile on
Your face when you
Are at a loss for words

I am mine before
I am yours
But
Still I lay my heart
In your hands because
It is yours as
Yours is mine

When I creep into your reverie
I hope you smile because
You think this time
For the first time
You finally got it right
You think this time
For the last time
You finally found forever

Tonight
I fall asleep alone
Wrapped in my
Own thoughts
Wishing I was wrapped
In your arms instead

I once was a mess
On the kitchen floor
You came along
And swept me up
Without realizing
Just what it meant

Maybe I shouldn’t
Revolve my days around
You
But the pull
Of your orbit is
Something I can’t help but
Let myself fall into

I’d run away with you if
You asked

I’ve been hurt and I’ve
Been used
So please
Be gentle and handle
With care
Because what I give
To you is yours
To keep

You touch me in a way only
You can you touch me and I
Know that everything will
Be ok

I just want to be ok

I like to point
Out my flaws before
Others can discover them
But with you
They don't exist

You did not teach me
How to love
I taught myself the moment
I looked in
And let go
But you reassured me that
What I felt was valid and
For once I could
Give in to someone fully

I used to believe I
Knew what unconditional love
Felt like but
Realized I was wrong
The moment your lips
Touched my soul

Somehow
Even in black and white
You fill my world
With color and remind
Me why we live with
Our eyes open

You made fire
Out of me when
I was nothing
More than ashes

Part 1

As we walked I
Counted the window panes
On the buildings we passed
One, two, three, four
One, two, three, four
You walked ahead and
I counted your footsteps
Sixty six, sixty seven, sixty eight
Sixty nine, seventy, seventy one

Part 2

The cold set in and I
Could see your breath as
It promised things unsaid
And in that moment
1,851 miles away from
Everything I know, I knew
I was home

I lost six hours when
I gave them to you
My feet were too
Heavy
My mouth weighed
Down by words
I couldn’t speak

Just the touch of
Your hand is enough
To heal even the
Darkest thoughts that
Cloud my mind

Watching the way your
Lips twitch between
Rises of your chest
Wondering:
Is it me you're
Dreaming of?

As you slept I
Watched the city lights
Twinkle below us like
Stars I knew
That this is what I wanted
Where I wanted to be
Always

I cried on my way
Home melting into
Every color of
The sunset brought on
By the allure you
Bring to my life and I was
Reminded
Why I stayed

When our lips touch I
Breathe you in
And it feels like
Everything
Is right again

Call me by your name
Let me know that
I'm yours to keep
In times when I
Doubt myself and need
Your touch let me know
That I'm yours
To keep

Maybe
It’s today maybe
It’s tomorrow
If you stick around I
Can show you what
Forever
Feels like

When the green light reflects
Off your eyes
With the taste of your
Skin under my teeth
I want to feel like this
For all of time with
You by my side with
You in my veins
So promise me you'll
Stick around with me
In this life and the next
Always

It's times like these that
I'm happy I have you to
Fill my heart with what's
Always been missing and
It's times like these that
I know I want to spend the
Rest of my time with you by
My side I know that I want
To create a life with you
Because
It's you that fills my mind,
My heart, my soul in times
That I can't feel them at all

In the constellations that cluster
My midnight sky you're
The star that shines brightest
And guides me back when I
Get lost in this every day life

I found the best
Parts of me in
All of you

And I know one
Day you'll break
My heart because that's
How love works just
Promise you'll do it
With gentle hands

Outside it’s pink and
Spring came so
Unexpectedly like how
You kissed me in
My bedroom so
Many months ago

I asked God where
I’m suppose to be I
Slept for years
Opened my eyes and
Woke up in
Your arms

May 22, 2017

I sat down today and
Cried thinking how cold
This world is but
I took solace in knowing
That my little piece of the
Universe is warm with
You in it

When you’re away does
Your body ache like
Mine does? When I hurt
Do you feel it? When
I’m distant and not present
Do you notice?
Or
Is it just me?

And I wonder why it
Is that when you're gone
I miss you more than you
Do me why it is that I
Hang on every word, every
Text waiting for contact when you
Arrive but I'm left waiting, wondering
Why it's me that cares
More

And I stay because you
Give me a reason to when the
World is against me and I
Hate myself but sometimes
I get weak and it gets hard so
All I ask is that you take my
Hand and help me through
My darkness because a
Love worth living for means
So much more than a
Love worth dying for

I’m too proud to say that
I’m afraid
That I might ruin this because
This is the best thing
I’ve had and
You deserve so much more
Than the mess that I
Bring to this world

The scariest thing in life is
Not to be left alone or even
A broken heart
The scariest thing in life is
To be loved and to be filled with
Love so fully that you know
Deep down
That you'll never be alone again

Sometimes I think of our
Love and cry
I know in some fucked up
Way that's not right
But our pasts aside I
Want you to know that in
You I have found myself I
Have found the purest and
Truest form of love that
Exhausts the soul into
Pure bliss in you I've found
My home

The things I feel are
Exciting and new but not
Because I've never felt
Love before but because
With you
Love feels raw and love
Feels real because with
You love makes sense and
That's the way it should be

Right now
Everything's tinted pink and
I don't know what to
Think
When I'm dancing in the
Rain to all the love songs
In my brain
That you sing to
Me on repeat

You
Are the
Only
One

With that being
Said I want you to
Know that in the deepest
Parts of my soul in the
Darkest crevices of my
Beating heart I know
That you're *The One*

He’s wild and free something
I’m not used to it scares
Me but I’m addicted
Like a thunderstorm on a
Hot summer’s day
I can’t help but dance
With the lightning
The raindrops like
His fingertips
Embracing me and soaking
Me to my bones

You spoke my name as
Easy as summer appeared
And you weren’t something
I was ready for
But you
Came so sweet to my life
Like honey on my lips

I want to be the
Only boy
You love for the
Rest of your life and
In return I
Promise to do the same

It’s the way your words
Spill out of your mouth
Each intonation and cadence
Delivered flawlessly during
Conversations in your car
Long past sundown with
Nothing but headlights on
Pavement in front of us rediscovering
What it means to be young and
In love

In this summer heat you've
Got me melting away
Sweet like ice cream
Under your touch
It engulfs me until you're
All I feel

You paint me up in
Shades of cool
Your fingers the brush you
Strip me down with your eyes until
I'm nothing more than
Art laying naked in
Front of you

These are
Just letters on a page
To fill the spaces between
What I can't seem to put
Into words and
What I try so desperately to

you still leave me
speechless

He’s gentle like love
Should be with tough hands
And a voice that could
Soothe even the most
Troubled soul

I’m small and I am
Soft but you hold me like
I’m fire
Wild and hot
Under your tongue

You came into my life
Unexpectedly
You weren't something
I was looking for yet
You took my love and
Left me yearning
For more

I’ve never asked for
Praise but I find you
On your knees
At my feet
Willing to please

In the stillness
Of my mind
In the silence
Between my teeth
In the moments that
I’m alone I think
Of you
And I know that I’ll
Never truly be alone

I’ve waited so long to
Be able to breathe that
I forgot how it felt
To not be so blue
Until you came along

Your love feels like ecstasy
Flowing through my veins keeping
Me just high enough that
I never touch the ground
And for once I’m not scared
To look down because I
Know you won’t let me fall

The roses you gave me
Expired weeks ago
But still
I keep them

As the sky blurs and begins
To wane into the night
Greens and blues
Jump alive with the last
Seconds of the fading light
From a day spent dreaming
About you

I’d give all my sunrises to
Spend all my sunsets
With you

You’ve built me from
The ground up like a
Statue from marble
A shrine
For all to see of a
God untouched

This life is not mine nor
Is it yours the
Day we met this life
Became ours to share
The day we met we
Became one soul shared
Between two bodies

When I hear that song it
Takes me back to when I
Danced around in nothing but
Your robe before the words we
Spoke became our truth

now playing:
dog years // maggie rogers

I
Love
You
More
Than
Anyone
I’ve
Ever
Loved

Alone
In this storm it’s cold and
I can’t distinguish my
Tears from the raindrops but
Still I walk to you because
You are the calm
In the eye of my hurricane

Just know that
When the words flow from
Your mouth like poison
I'll still be here in the morning

With you I know that no
Matter where we are or
Where we go we’ll
Always be home
Because

With you life is
Like a never ending house
Party endlessly spinning through
Room after room
Dancing the night away
Intoxicated by nothing but
Each other's presence

Spent the day
On the floor
And smiled
Because I thought
Of you

we've come full circle

I took a chance and
Gambled on you
My time
My happiness
My love but I
Knew in the end I would
Win because I never start
Something I could lose

The first winds of autumn
Have come and it reminds
Me of when I
First started to fall

I know with you I
Don't have to work
Overtime
To stay on your mind
Because this is different

9 to 5

I'll continue to dance in
Crowds full of strangers
In places new to us both
Spinning around to the words
You whisper in the dark because
You paint the night with such
Beautiful colors

Maybe it's the drugs
That my heart produces
Pumping through my veins
Reaching every part of my body
That keeps me dancing to
The words that you sing

When we dance I can feel you
Under my fingertips speaking of
The things you're afraid
To say of the things you
Hang your hopes on:
Me

As your fingertips glide
Gently over the freckles the
Sun has ever so generously graced
Me with for once I can say
I'm sad to see summer come
To an end

I’m desperate to breathe
You in every second of
Every day

I never thought
I would need another
Until you found your way
Inside me

You remind me of all the
Places I’ve ever longed for
Warm and safe

I tuck you in with words
That hang from my lips
The same words that once
Hid behind my teeth the
Same words that get stuck
Under my tongue but somehow
You pull them out so painlessly

It’s funny
How your eyes light up when
You see me or how you think I
Don’t notice when you steal glances
At me when we’re driving in your car
It’s funny because
No one has ever seen me
In the same light
Your eyes find me in

I sometimes wish
That I could be
Half as good of a person
As you are but what I lack
You make up for

And then
I realize that for you
I do the same

The moment I stopped chasing
The thing I wanted most
Was the moment
You found me

Of all the possibilities in
This world I get
To be yours

I was never one
For much but I’ve
Always been a sucker
For your love

I was always guarded with
My heart
My love careful and calculated
But you came along with a
Promise and a determination
To never let this go
To never let me go
To never let *us* go

Your love slips over
Me warm and gentle like the
Embers from a dying fire
Of another life

I don't mind when you
Talk over my favorite songs because
Your voice is the sweetest tune
I've ever heard

In you I
Lose my days and
I hope I never
Get them back

You planted your love deep
In the crevices of my heart your
Roots spread wide like
The arms you wrap around me

You planted roses in the cracks
Of my ribs and watched as
They blossomed
Filling my lungs with the most
Beautiful air

take my thorns with
my petals

I'd give you the moon and
All her stars
I'd give you the sun and
All her warmth
Just to keep
That smile on your face
Because it is the beauty that
Keeps my universe together

I fall weak for your hands
When they find their way
Around my neck

I never cared to play with
Others but when we’re
Side by side
Shoulder to shoulder
In your room I know that
I’ve found my Player 2

And I know that if I let
You capture my heart it’d
Be game over for me

I don't say this enough
But thank you
For everything you do
Thank you

Your body was carved
From gold
Each curve mighty like
A mountain each stretch mark
A badge of honor from the battles
You've waged all your life and
I promise to kiss and praise each
One until the war is over
And every day thereafter

The mornings I wake up alone
I still seem to find you
Intertwined in my sheets your
Scent lingering on my skin and
I smile knowing that one day I'll
Never have to wake up
Alone again

And I run
From what I do not know
But
What I do know is that
At the end of this race when
I’m tired and my lungs no longer
Fill with air
I’ll find you waiting for me with
Open arms and a gentle embrace

I love it when you
Speak my name because
It’s never tasted so
Delicious on anyone else’s
Tongue

Your smile still
Makes my heart
Skip a beat

The butterflies have turned
To earthquakes

For me it's
A
L
W
A
You
S

You took each piece of my broken
Heart into your hands and
Kissed them softly mending
Them back together with the
Finest gold that flowed from
Your lips knowing
That now it would be
All yours

Your touch could
Rival that of
Midas

You never took me as damaged
Goods you never accepted that I
Was less than what I am
You took me as
I was and gave me time

The greatest
Gift you've ever
Given me
Is patience

I needed to change my
Perspective to see that the world
Couldn’t be all that bad if
You’re in it

Your peach is the sweetest
Fruit I’ve ever
Tasted

The stars shine brighter
Now that you're in
My universe

I don’t want to *need*
You but I **do**

One year
Has passed one year
Has come and gone the
Seasons changed and still
You’re here

I lay my body in
Front of you every mark
And flaw to see so
Why don't you take it?

devour me, babe

The night we met
Was the moment my
Life began
The stars aligned
And I think the
Universe knew

I want to always remember
The way you looked the night
You told me you loved me
Because I've never seen
Someone look so beautiful

No one mapped this life out
But I don’t mind
Being lost
Just as long as
I’m lost with you

great adventures await us

It’s when your tongue is
Between my legs that I
Learned to pray to a god
I don’t know
Thanking him for the
Words you whisper in the dark

When you forget
I’ll be here to remind you
You’re gorgeous, love

I like the way you take
Every inch of me in with
Nothing but your lips until
You find the spot
Where my body stops
And heaven begins

If you asked me to
Spend the rest of my life
With you
As yours
I’d say yes and I know that
Should scare me but it
Doesn’t because with you the
Future doesn’t scare me at all

I’m ready

It’s been so long now since I’ve first
Felt your touch and still you’re
The only thing that races through my
Mind and
Sometimes I sit by my window and
Stare at the stars wondering how it is you’re
The center of my universe
All my suns and all my moons and
Every constellation in between

When I look down I still see
Your hand in mine even when the
Spaces between my fingers are empty

It’s cold now and still
I find myself reaching for you
In the dark still
I find myself yearning for your
Touch yearning for your brown eyes
Warm like whisky down my throat

I don’t think you realize or
Maybe you just don’t know but
On that September night
You arrived just in time
To save what little love was
Left in my world

Press me between your pages
Like a flower long forgotten
Because this love is my
Favorite fairytale

From time to time
When I can remember I
Try to walk a little slower because
I was rushing through life
Before I met you now it's all I can do
To make the moments last
With you
I don't want to miss a thing

It's like a funky love song stuck
In your head or a crackling bonfire on a
Cold, dark night it's familiar yet
New and exciting and each taste you
Get you want just a bit more
That's our love

I woke up to a whisper ever so
Quiet I almost missed it but the
Secrets it held were for me and
Me alone
Thank you for loving him
And to that I replied
Always

she's still here

Your face is like heaven and
When it’s cradled in my palms
I know I have the whole world
In my hands

I knew you were The
One when you looked into my
Eyes and I no longer felt like
I had anything to hide like I
No longer had a reason to
Run

I’m the luckiest person
Because I get to call you
Home

my four leaf clover

I promise to love you long
After the party ends

You touch me and I am nothing
More than soft skin exposed
Exploding into a thousand different
Stars under your fingertips

I never have to question
His love
Because
I feel it
Even when we’re apart

Whether you stay or leave my
World will never be the same

If my words hold true it’s
Easy to say
You’re the love of my
Life

The nights when the sun
Sets on your skin I swear I
Can see the sun rise the
Next morning in your eyes

This might be the end
Of this chapter
But for us
It’s just the beginning because
I could never run out of
Words about you

I’ve said this many times
Now but I love you
Always

Made in the USA
Middletown, DE
24 July 2020